Logical Topologies
part 1

By Dr. Sotiria Theoharis

Contents

Social Spaces and Universes as Three-Dimensional and Complex

1. <u>Social Spaces (De)centered from Absolute zero.</u>

The (de)centered world is a reality needed for some problems. The world is (de)centered from the point of "absolute zero."[1] It is relatively centered from other points in the field where a relative axial system can be defined as placed through the center of each sematic universe. The point of absolute zero is where matter is frozen out of which new worlds can manifest and old worlds fall or fail into.[2] The relative center is defined for computational purposes in the next section. We operate under a relative center. We live in relative numbers not absolute ones as it is

---

[1] Absolute zero is like zero Kelvin in temperature, where matter freezes. It is possible that that is true everywhere in the universe or it could be true for the earth sphere only.

[2] See Gilles Deluze. (1993). Leibniz. (1998). The argument on nature is interesting since the world is not it's mechanical idol.

hard to define meaning from the edges and corners of the semantic social universe or from the outside in-looking. There is an imaginary outside, which can be stretched to be included in the semantic universe. This imaginary outside comes at a defined phase from the absolute.

Let's for all practical purposes imagine an edge or line of flight and imagine it collapsing at absolute zero. Absolute zero is physically outside the realm of the thought universe at some large maybe even infinite number of relative known semantic units. Maybe those can be computed as one shifts perspective from large to small universes from the end to the beginning of processes.

A semantic unit is a minimum unit of meaning in terms of length, height, or width as defined by the terms in the semantic universe at hand. In my example, "Life with breast cancer: Timing Medical Intervention", a unit of breast cancer risk is defined at this moment, when it can be potentially identified on a mammographic plate prior to self-exam and prior to clinical exam. Thus, it is the earliest unit of defined risk and is the earliest finding on a plate for said cancer. Genetic testing may be a slightly earlier position for defined material risk, but that is still in dispute. Self-exam or clinical breast exam may be defined for others as the earliest material risk sighting.

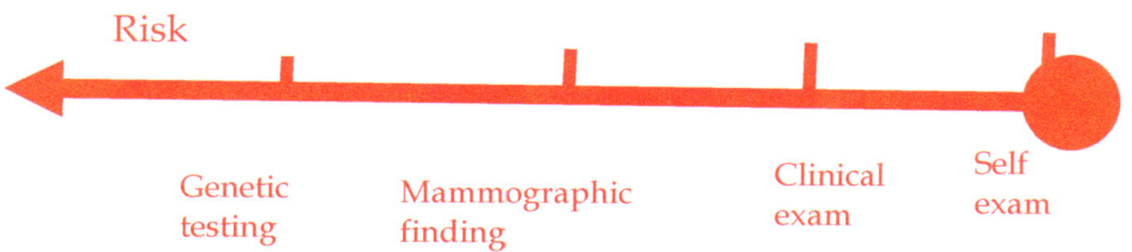

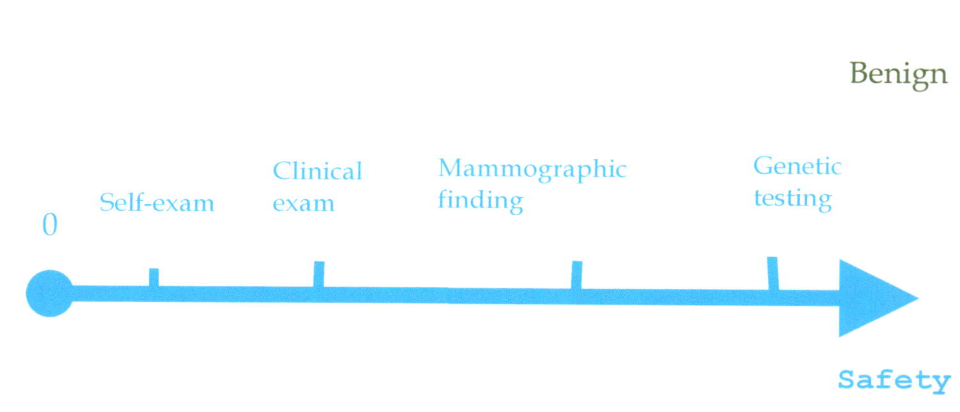

So, when you are safe, you don't find a lump

in the self-breast exam or clinical exam, and

you see on the mammographic plate something

benign instead of cancerous or when your genes

are defined as genetically benign. At risk

means that there is a finding of concern

(almost cancer or cancer) in self-exam,

clinical exam, mammographic plate or genetic

testing. Late means that cancer is relatively

metastasized not in situ. Trust unit means

that we are at ease with medical care we

receive. Fearful means that we are uneasy with

the medical care we receive. Now that I have

defined semantic units, let me imagine the

place as whole again, from the point of view

of absolutes. The world our earth is the

physical example. The current advances in the

gravity field show how complex our

understanding is. Here is an image of the

earth and its gravitational field.[3]

---

[3] From **sharing earth observatory research**, on an image from the gravitational field research non-earth probe. It is credited to Stanford University.

At absolute zero from outside or at the membrane of the word, all lines meet and they are parallel and/or bent, by the parameters of normal geometric space. I imagined 6 such corners represented by grey rhombuses for 3 d space. These are the absolute zeroes of the sematic world of thought [speculative dark (w)holes] that envelope the world. The world recedes as you in-look. It extends as you out-look.[4]

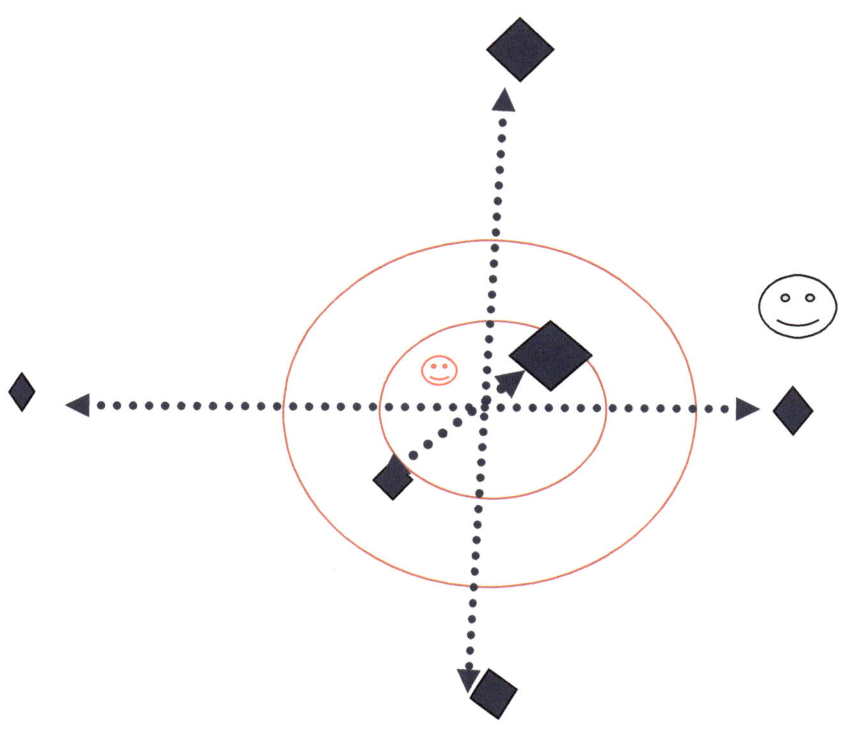

Let us imagine at least 6 such absolute directions in space, which could be connected in a system of absolute zero's or dark (w)holes, these contain a practical defined

---

4 The graph is meant to illustrate not handicap your vision of the universe. I speculate the universe has the shape of a sphere. The lines represent the axial system we could image the universe rotating and operating with.

infinity and are represented by the dark rhombuses or membranes.

In a 2d cross-section, such world is bound 4 2 d axial systems, which we could conceive of as simultaneous. We could picture an axial system going through the world. This axial system is dependent on the world, its space and conditions are relative measurements. The corners of the world are defined in terms of absolute (outside) zeroes. The corners are a relative infinity away from relative (inside) 0. The two axes go through the center or a known defined point inside the thought world. The parabolas are the outside lines or membrane field lines which bend to parallel though virtually perpendicular to the axes, if continued at a defined phase.

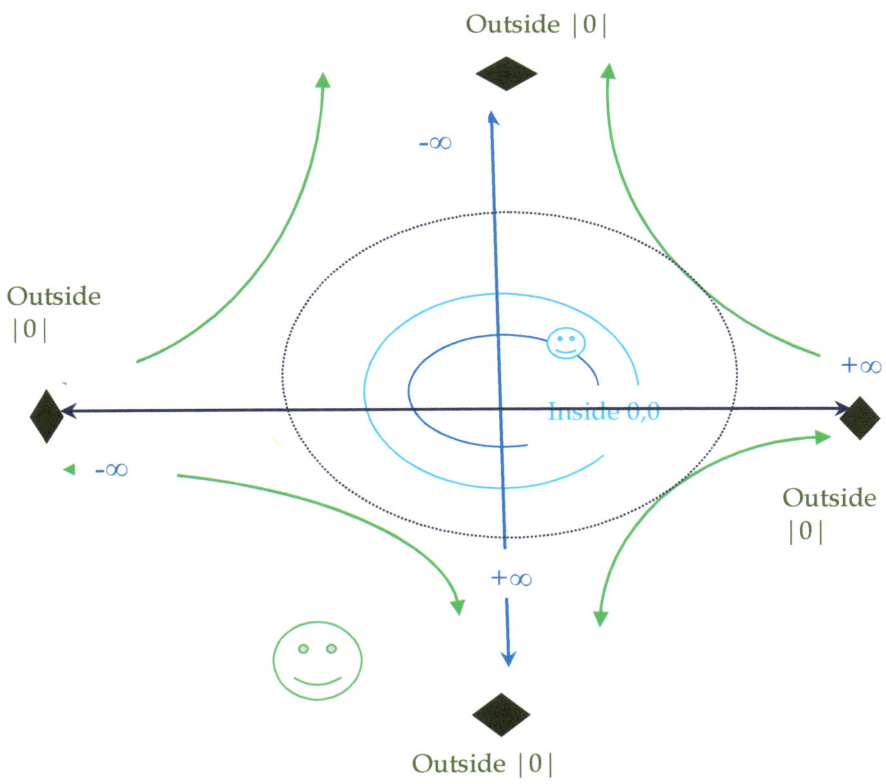

Outside |0|
Outside |0|
Outside |0|
Outside |0|
-∞
+∞
-∞
+∞
Inside 0,0

2. A Practical decentered worldview an example.

Let me define how we could use a practical example for the centered world view. Let us imagine the breast cancer world as it is centered on the concepts early-late, trust-fear, security-risk like in my study "Life with breast cancer: Timing Medical Intervention." The lines of flight or positive edges are defined as the following.

Example: we arrive outside a positive infinity of security and outside negative infinity of risk when we imagine absolute zero risk. This means there is no relative risk at all. Absolute zero risk refers to infinitely positive early interventions and infinitely negative late interventions. Absolute zero risk depends on a positive infinity of trust and a negative infinity of fear. Absolute zero further risk isn't a life possibility. It exists in the stasis and finitude of terminal diagnosis or death from the disease or from successful avoidance and recovery from the disease to other causes of death. Life is represented by the green circle that reseeds or extends depending on the diagnosis. It is my belief that we can successfully surpass this disease like others[5] through prayer.

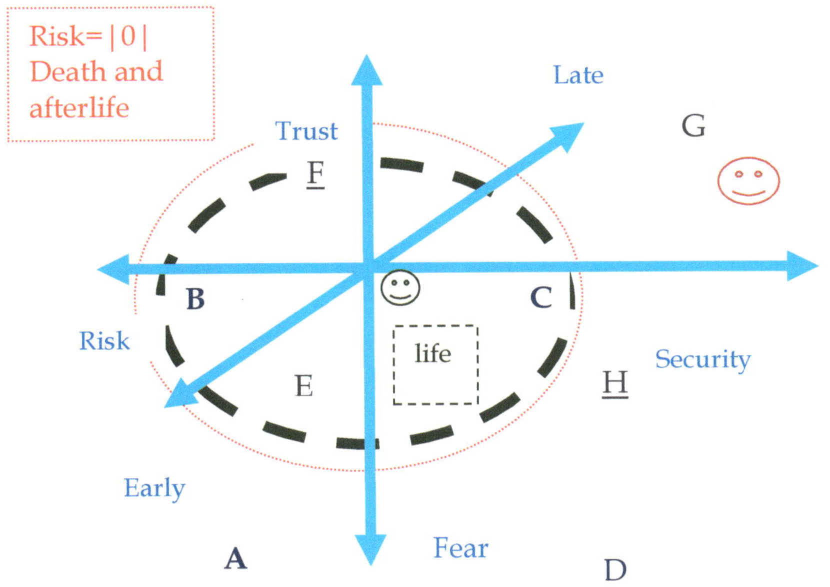

---

[5] We can transcend our death and life on earth and have eternal life.

Let me explain absolute zero risk. If we are
at 100% risk or infinite risk we are suffering
from the disease and most likely perish from
it. Thus, we are not able to further suffer
from it. 100% late means we likely perished
from the disease and cannot further suffer
from it. 100% early means that we caught it
before it materialized as a possibility so we
are not at risk for it. 100% fear means we
cannot possible fear more. No further risk
could shake us. 100% trust we could overcome
any instance of risk and are not shaken.

3. <u>Social Spaces as Physical, Mathematical, Metaphysical Centered Spaces</u>

Hypothesis: A social space is defined by an axial system that is relatively centered. It is centered relatively in the defined origin of the semantic social world at hand. This can be at a defined phase or angle. The center of the semantic world is dependent on the conditions of the world not in numerical absolutes. It is a mathematical space, a physical space, and a metaphysical one too.

Social space is physical in so far as a microphysics of action and interaction can be defined. Social space is mathematical in so far as abstract or linguistic and numerical symbols can be used to define it. In social space, we can calculate the chance of social events occurring. We can define the geometric parameters of spaces and subspaces. Social space is metaphysical in so far as a momentum of events (a speeding up or slowing down) occur in such space. In logical social spaces, mathematical events occur and can be quantified and qualified. Let me illustrate.

In my study of breast cancer care, "Life with Breast Cancer: Timing Medical Intervention" I found that Trust is opposite Fear, Risk to Security and Late timing to Early timing. Thus, an individual directs or orients spiritually or psychologically- in the metaphysical system, materially and logistically- in the physical system, numerically and logically- in the mathematical system. The social space or terrain is defined materially, logically, and spiritually by these parameters from the inside out.

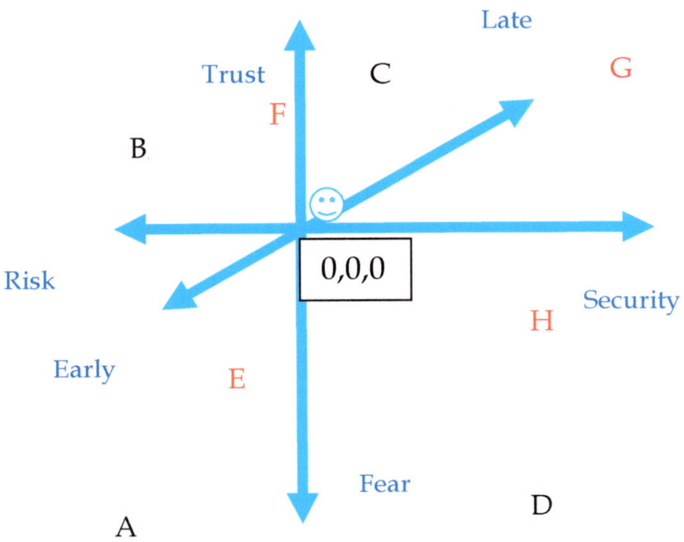

The social space that is defined by this axial system is logical. It is defined by classifying areas of intervention. There are eight logical operative quadrants in this description.

A. Medical Intervention that is defined as risky, early and based on fear.

B. Medical intervention that is defined as
   risky, early and based on trust.

C. Medical intervention that is defined as
   safe, early and based on trust.

D. Medical Intervention that is defined as
   safe, early and based on fear.

E. Medical intervention that is based on
   risk, fear and late.

F. Medical intervention that is based on
   risk, trust and late.

G. Medical intervention that is based on
   safe, trust, and late.

H. Medical intervention that is based on
   safe, fear, and is late.

These logical spaces define the areas an
individual can move physically,
intellectually, and psychically in relative
social space. The job of the sociologist is to

define by how much and in what manner the movement occurs in each direction physically, mentally and spiritually. The problem becomes that of visualizing and conceptualizing sociology along the lines of physical-material, mathematical-logical and spiritual-psychological spaces. How these spaces materialize in actions is key! We imagine it as a social physical space-game.

Sotiria Theoharis
23/3/2017 "Breast Care"
Breast Care Clinic

4. <u>Why do social axial systems exist and how many are there?</u>

First hypothesis social space is fundamentally three dimensional, orthogonal, and contiguous with physical space.[6] In fact, objects in socio-physical space have their own axial system to define them well. Two objects may share a social-physical axial system or have an overlapping/ overarching axial system. Social-physical axial systems exist to define objects and subjects in physical-(time centered), mathematical- (computation or calculus centered), and metaphysical (momentum centered) spaces.

---

[6] Adele Clarke (2005) has argued for a 2 D model.

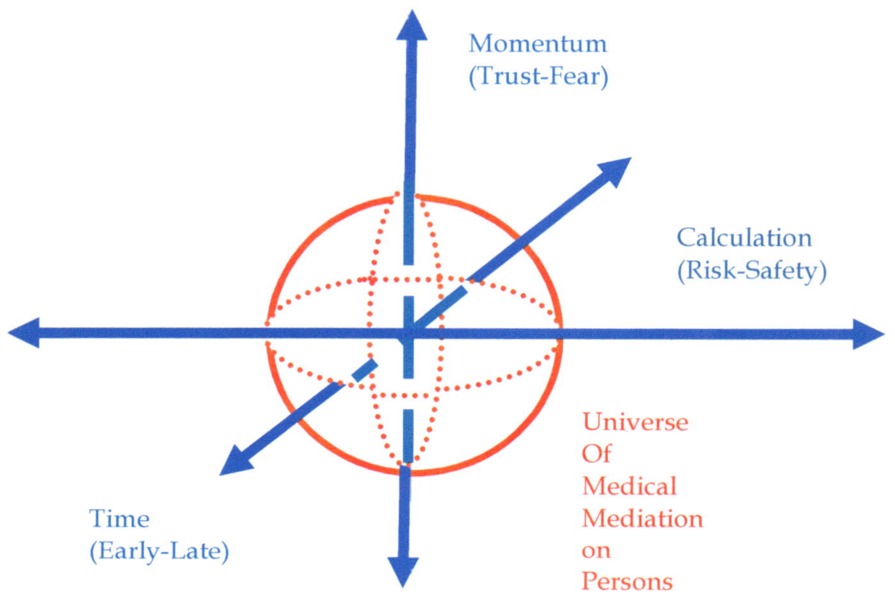

Piloting the Universe of Medical Mediation on Persons (UMMP), the patient/ person uses his or her own subjective axial system and universe. Those are support/ estrangement, responsibility/ blame, comply (liberty)/ not-comply (unfreedom). The personal actions take place in the Universe of Persons in Medicine (UPM). These actions are internal, external and spiritual.

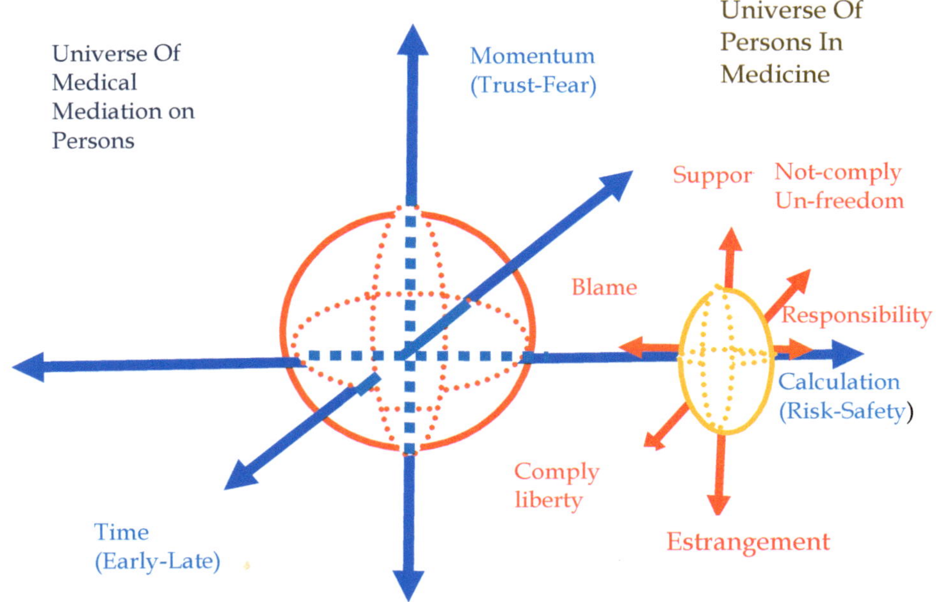

Blame/ responsibility is an internal calculation gauge. Support/ estrangement is a manifest spiritual gauge. Comply (liberty) and not comply (unfreedom) is an external physical gauge. This secondary social axis system helps illuminate those processes, which in combination is the golden sphere of the universe of persons subject to medicine.

The dependent or secondary axial systems could be equivalent to as many persons involved in medical care as a social space as rational collectives or discrete individuals. Thus, the number of dependent axial systems is equivalent to persons and collectives of persons involved. I consolidate an axial system across such persons based on their statements. [7]

In this regard, clarifying statements helps clarify positions in the axial system of the collective, which has so many variables. I speculate that axial systems are a factor of 3d in sociology that we work in 3 d spaces and sub spaces as we are living beings in such rational orthogonal worlds.[8] Discourse itself is necessarily 3D not only as a mode of

---

[7] Foucault. (1972). *Archeology*.

[8] Descartes. (1985). *The philosophical writings of Descartes*.

representation a word or book, but as a

material effect as it represents and

manipulates rationally and faithfully an

existing complex 3D world.

Social Space and the Medical Universe

1. Medical organization and social universe

A medical organization is a key place where you see how the social and the physical co-reside occupying 3 dimensional worlds. I have established how the axial coding of worlds is necessarily 3 D: spiritual-psychological, physical-social, and mathematical-logical. There are worlds and sub-worlds, universes and part-universes. Universes are larger and 3D still. Sub-worlds also are 3D. There are overlapping worlds.[9] If we define the universe of medical action in a hospital as the most inclusive world of social action in the hospital, then sub-worlds are those that include action in the hospital of lower order for example the sub-world of surgery in a conventional hospital is

---

[9] See Adele Clarke for a different version.

different from the world of the hospital in total. The sub-world of hospital surgery is included in the hospital though it may have external links from the hospital through the universe of surgery.

The universe as well as the world is not flat even in discourse. It has physical dimensions to operate on the known world, to materialize. Well how do we start understanding the world and mapping out it's contours? I think the key is to understand the world and sub-word dimensions and to sort out relative physical influences just like you would do in a biological -physical system.

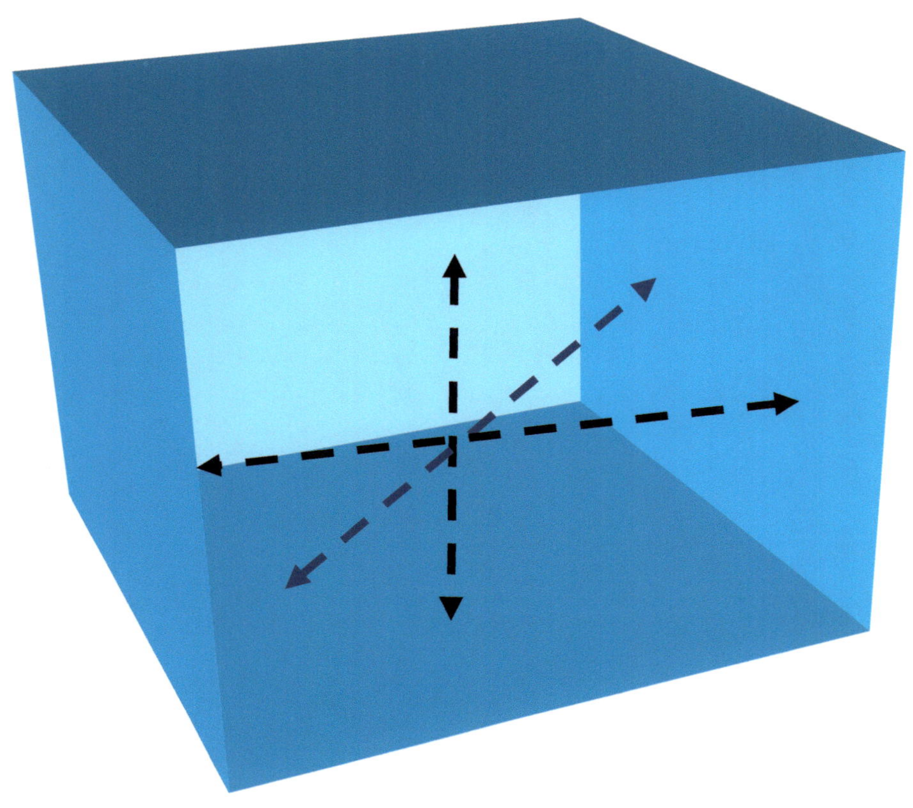

The universe contains the dimensions that compose it. I speculate for simplicity. The universe of medical action is like a cube. The actual shape is to be known. It is a complex volume that is dynamic. Not different from the physical world we inhabit. The architecture of

the world is complex as the flow of nature
tends to be overall complex. Sometimes it is
chaotic. Sometimes it is periodic. Sometimes
it is rhythmic. Sometimes it is static.
Sometimes dynamic. Sometimes it is simple.
The universe of medical action in a hospital
is a mixture of all those kinds of simple
worlds. Order is always evident and manifest
in all the phenomena as it is a sign of God.

The universe of medical events that happens
in a hospital tends to be over-all more
complex and needs to be managed to simplified
events that then beccme more streamlined and
manageable. Protocols exist to simplify and
streamline all contingencies and emergencies.

What does it mean for the world of medical
phenomena to be Simple, complex or chaotic?
Periodic, regular, or rhythmic? Static, fixed,
or dynamic? In the dimensions that follow:

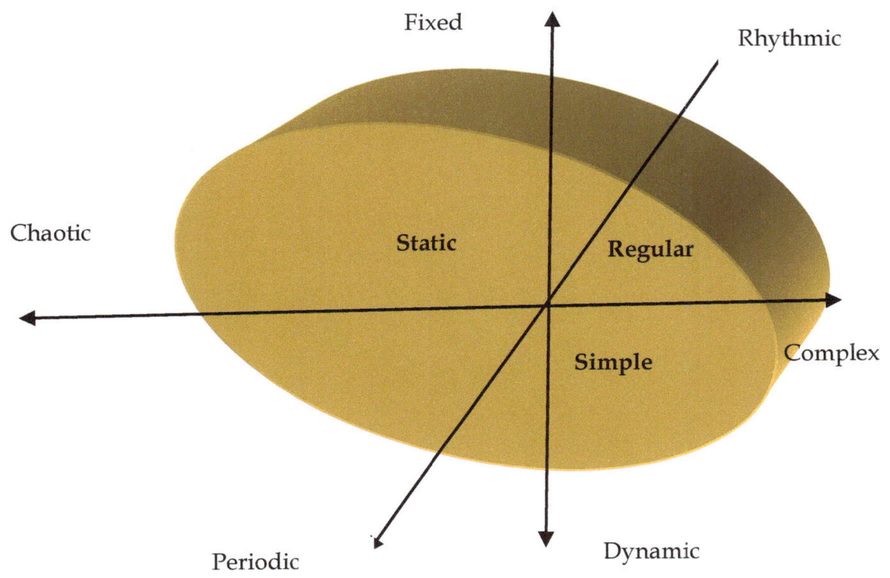

As we understand the map of medical phenomena, the world tends to be complex when a positive infinity of phenomena occurs, which we know how to handle. It becomes chaotic when a negative infinity of phenomena occurs, which are difficult or unknown how to handle. When events periodically occur, they are interesting and positive as they allow for proper intervention and anticipation. When

events occur out of the blue, they tend to
have regularity and a rhythm to be found
(incidence data).

  2. Medical-Social spaces

   The desire for medical order and coherence
is the key in proceeding. A complete social
space is naturally ordered. Human ordering is
necessary to the divine intelligence that
manifests in events. We are the humans that
manifest God's intelligent plan on the earth.
The medical-social space is divinely inspired
as it is cogent in all its complexity and
beauty. People desire to help others to be
cured and cared. They build intelligent modern
institutions. The medical institution sits in
a space that is first and foremost physical in
nature. It is a building, an architecture, an
enclosure that is carefully created to house

temporary the ill as they progress to health
under a care and cure worlds. [10]

The medical institution is born to care
and cure the ill. Medicine needs social
thinking and management science to create such
a world for people: a world that is a wellness
center not just a house for the ill. Medical
space is defined in breast care by the
parameters of its paradigm. The paradigm is
ordered through breast care prevention/
detection and therapeutics.

---

[10] Rise (1999) *Saving Bodies, Saving Souls.*

	Detection practice	Providers	Technology	Body-Part
1.	Self exam	Self or Lover	Hands Touch	Breast
2.	Clinical and Family History	Clinicians: Expert Nurses, General Practitioners	Discourse Pedigree	Self Breast Lineage
3.	Clinical Breast exam	Clinicians: Expert Nurses, General Practitioners	Expert hands Palpation	Breast
4.	Mammography Ultrasound MRIs	Radiologists Imaging technicians	Mammograms Ultrasound MRI	Breast
5.	Genetic testing	Genetic counselors, Geneticists, and lab technicians	Gene assay Discourse	Blood
6.	Biopsy Needle aspiration Lumpectomy Minor surgery	Surgeons Pathologists	Needles, dyes, microscope, surgical instruments	Tissue

Here there are dimensions as well in the
overlaying worlds. In the detection world for
example we move from less invasive to more
invasive procedures: from self-exam to clinical

and family history, to clinical exam, to
mammography or ultrasound or MRI, to genetic
testing, to biopsy/ needle aspiration/ and
lumpectomy. As a 3-d world, it is thus:

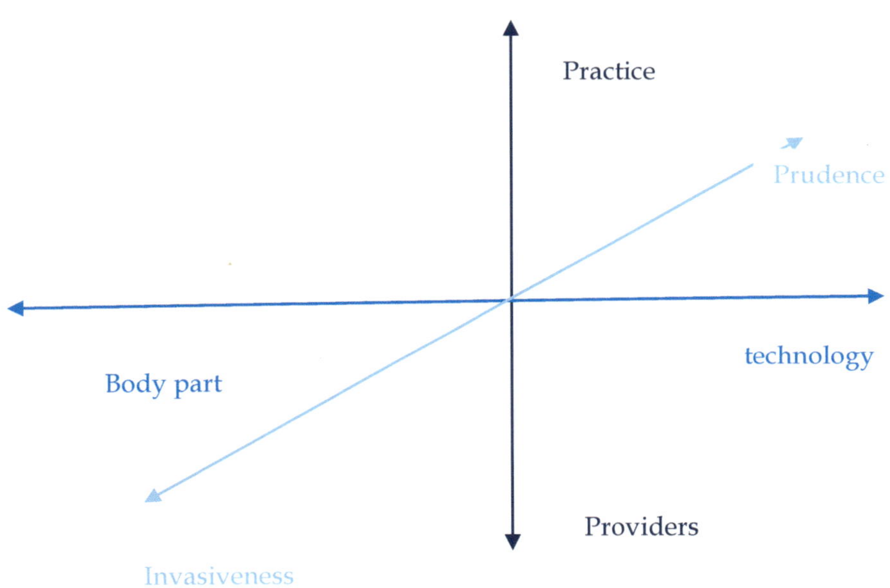

Let's take talk about this axial system so that
we are satisfied that it is orthogonal: not
Invasiveness is Prudence, not prudence is
invasiveness; not organic body-part is

technology, not technology is organic body part; Not provider is practice and not practice is provider.

Body part under examination can be the whole body to part of the body. The table suggests that we commonly use:

Body Part AXIS: large to small

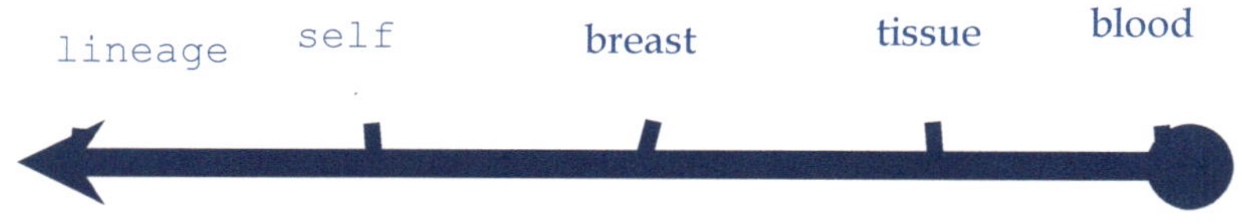

It is a cogent line from lineage and self to tissue and blood. Now let's look at the more crowded technology line.

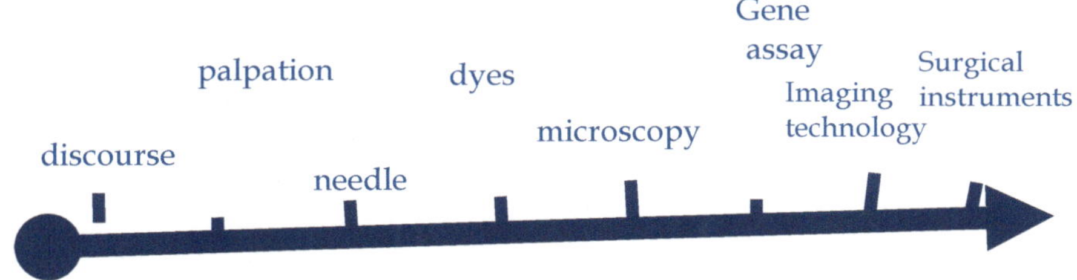

This line is harder to order but follows the reasoning simple to complex roughly. Let me order for you the Practice/ Provider lines.

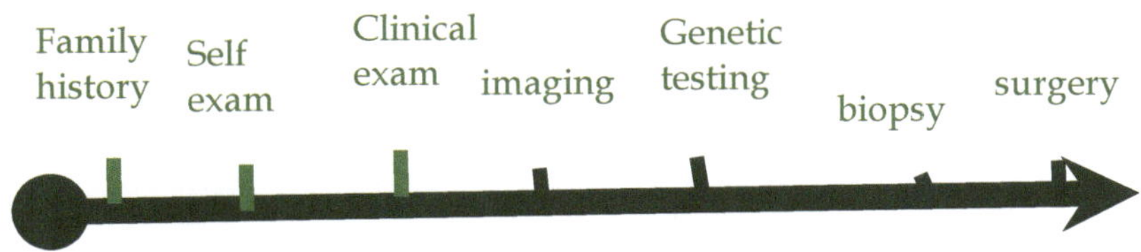

For the Practice line, we move from simple to complex. The provider line is similar. The reasoning follows frcm lay to expert.

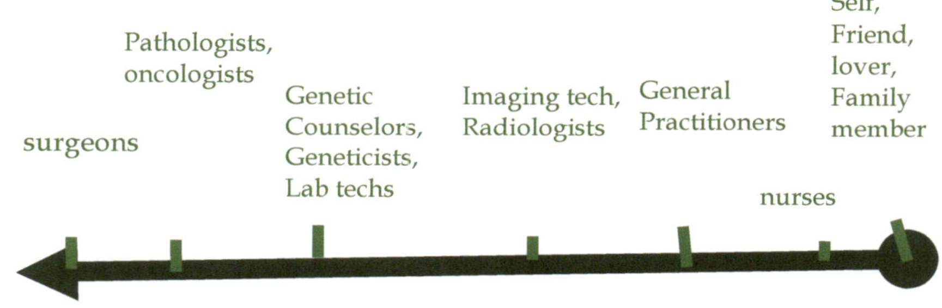

For Invasiveness to prudence the axial lines are basically defined based on need for further inquiry.

Invasiveness AXIS: simple to complex

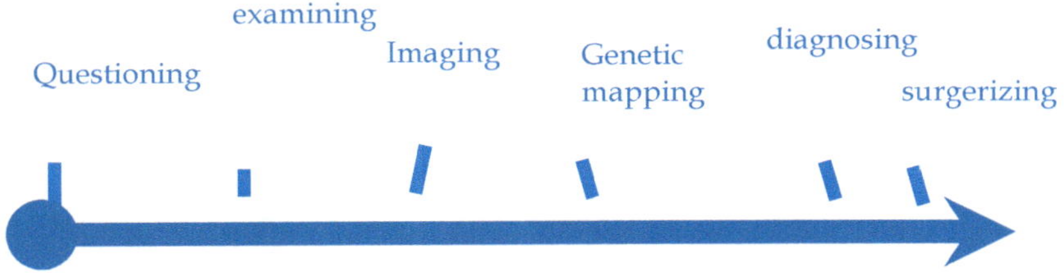

Here it is clear that invasiveness refers to

activities in medicine. Prudence also refers

to activities of caring for the self, mind and

body.

Prudence AXIS: Simple to
complex.

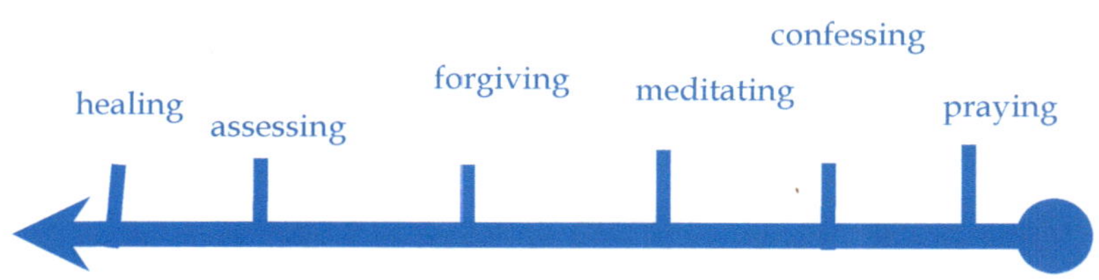

Prudence is the natural process of healing
which is a miracle of life. Let me look at how
we act in this world. I will map out a basic
trajectory.

3. Acting in Medical Diagnostic Social space

When a person acts in medicine, they move
through a simple to complex social, medical

and religious space. We must examine how they act in my topological model. We have the world of medical diagnostic practice and model that is based on Halsted's medicine. The model is summarized as following table which is an advance from my dissertation:

Early as opposed to late	Radical as opposed to conservative	Benign as opposed to cancerous
Defines operable/ inoperable cancers	Extent of surgery	Type of cancer
Defined local/ metastatic growth	Style of surgery	Spread of cancer
Times cancer onset for intervention	A paradigm of intervention	Defines operable
Grounds social definition of success	Criterion for successful operations	Enables successful intervention
Grounds medical policy	Grounds surgical authority	Enables action
Orders diagnosis/ detection	Orders sequence/ style of treatments	Enables care/ cure
Mobilizes women	"Debilitates" or "saves" women	Categorizes women

This table can be ordered as following worlds. Each row is conceivably a world. I will outline only 4. The space of the medical surgeon:

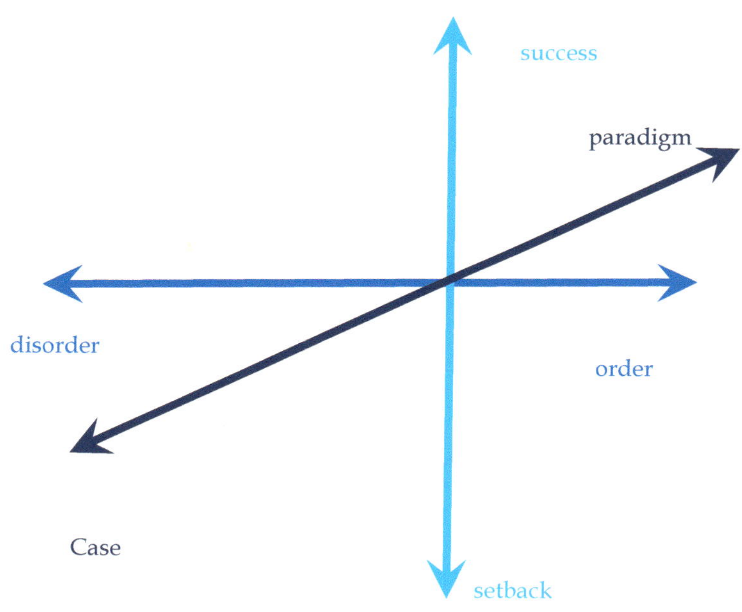

For the space of surgery, the following space is outlined:

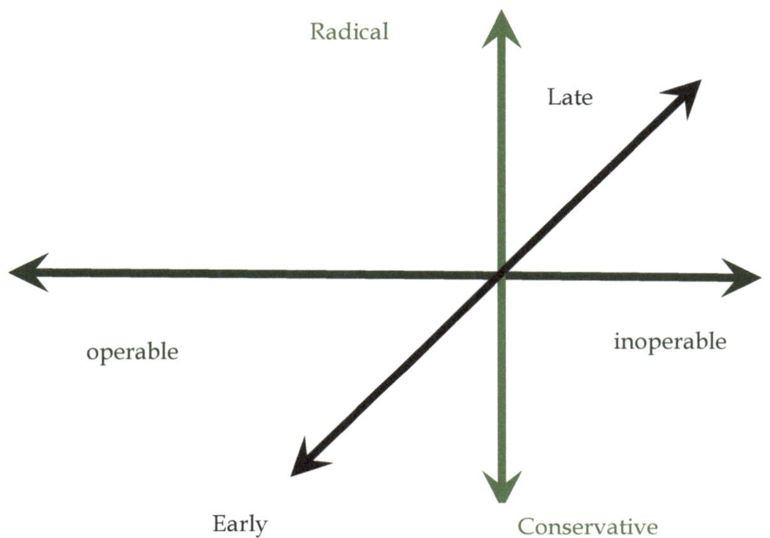

The space of diagnosis which is outlined
as 3D as well.

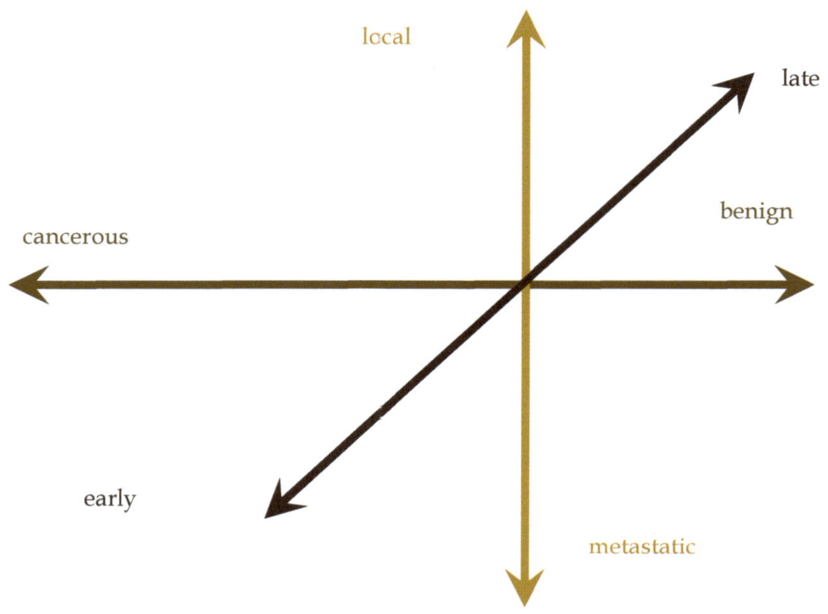

The world of the patient is also ordered though axial coding.

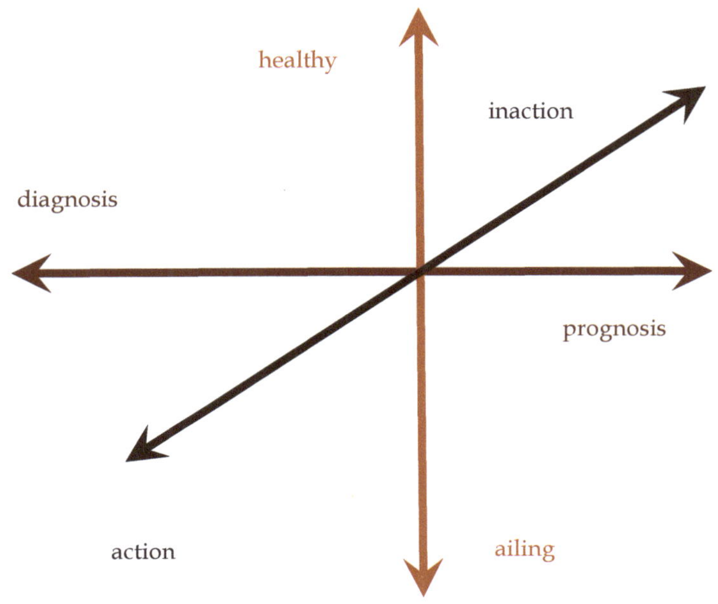

The space of medical care is thus more ordered. I will look at the care and cure worlds that are implied. The patient and physician can act in these words and become healthy depending on their personal status and case. The patient has clear trajectories though these spaces and so does the physician, the disease and the diagnoses. Let me outline the patient-world as I have patient data.

4. Care and Cure worlds

First let's look at the medical social sphere overall and put some values for the individual patient. For the patient, I have outlined the world which handles the paradigm and his or her heath. Let us closely define these axes.

A healthy person is based on the medical paradigm for the cure of breast cancer, which is based on the diagnosis and treatment of cancer. For patients, health rather than ailment is a key axis. I will illuminate it.

Healthy AXIS: physical to spiritual

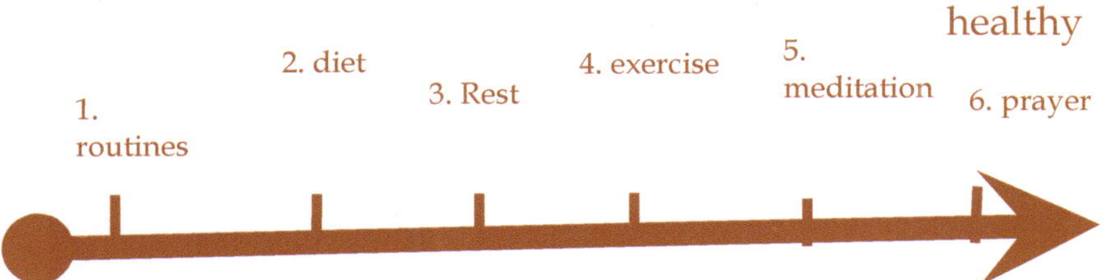

Ailing axis: physical to spiritual

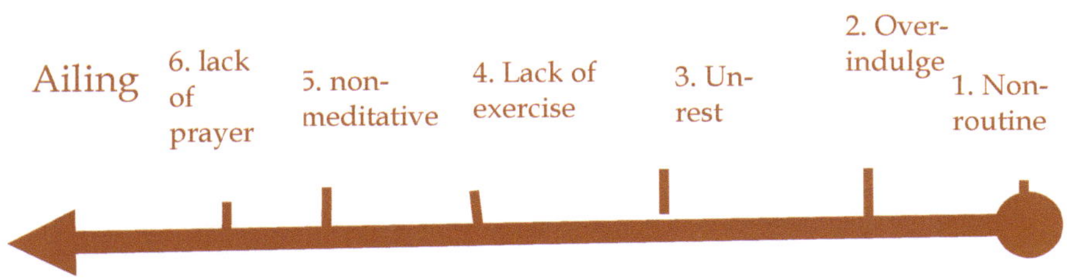

The next axis orders patients or persons in care/ cure world: the diagnosis/ pro-gnosis axis. Here pro-gnosis I mean what we may forecast based on diagnosis. Diagnosis means the actual event of benign to malignant cancer, normal to pathological.[11]

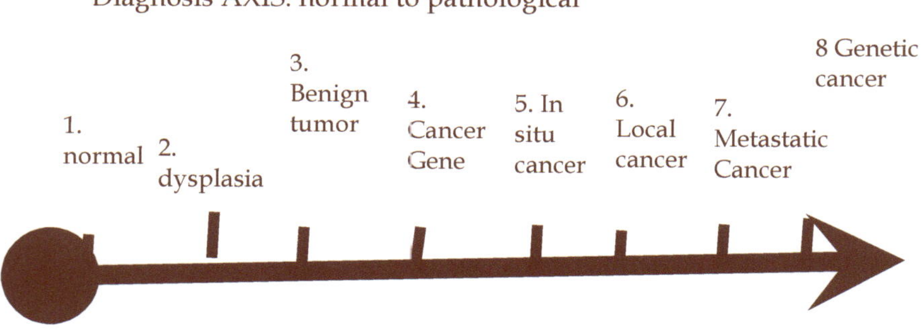

The prognosis axis helps establish what medical knowledge thinks is the life expectancy after diagnosis.

---

[11] See Canguilhem (1991).

Prognosis AXIS: healed to decline

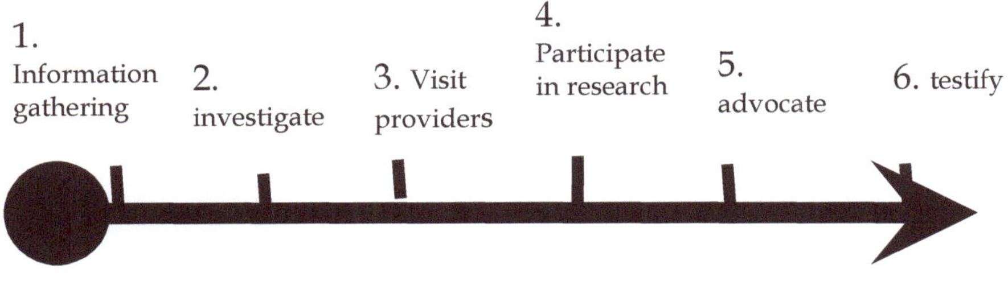

The action/ inaction line is the last key axis for the patient space. This is key to activate the patient to care for him/ her self.

Action AXIS: personal to political

The next and final axis is inaction of patient.

Inaction AXIS: passivity to immobility

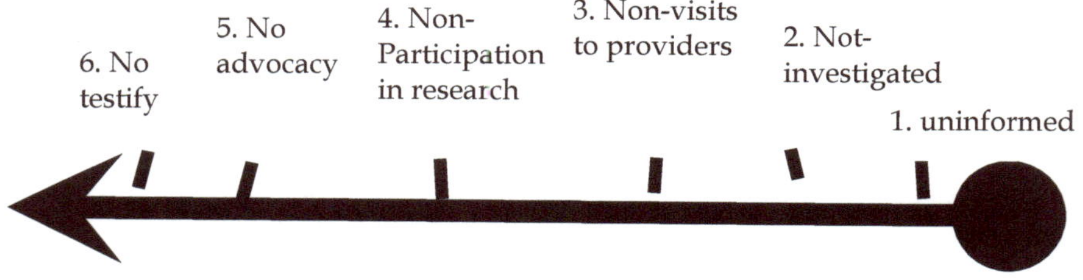

Patient trajectories are defined in the coordinated space. I will give one example before I close this section. Let us imagine that we have a patient who has completed the following numbers in care/ cure worlds.

I will pick a healthy person who is praying regularly (6), who is normal (1) who testifies

regularly in congress (6). Let me map the
position.

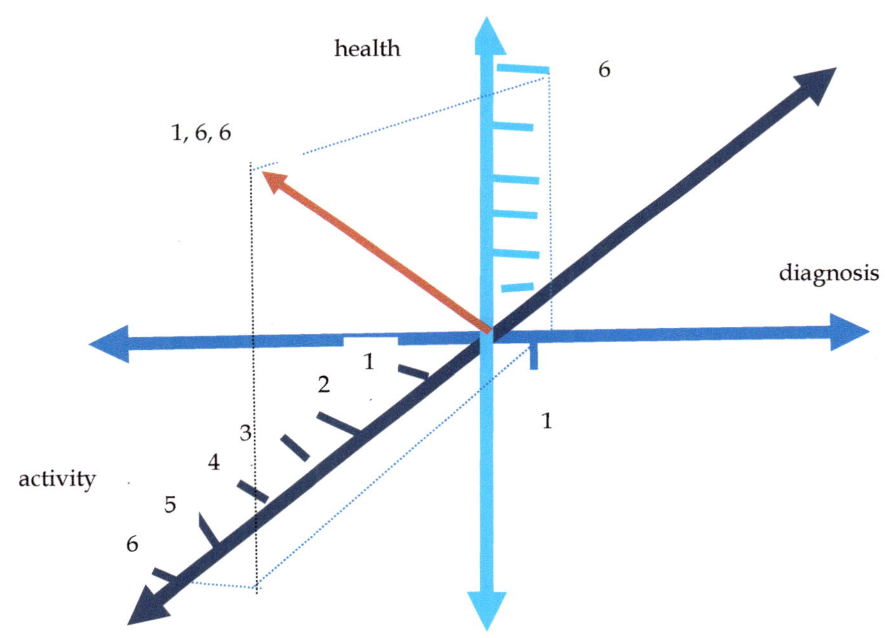

This chart illustrates that the axes can
be used in cohort. Overall, it is not just a
vector that we are looking at but a range of
values. I drew just the positive values. This
is due to chart simplicity.

This method is useful in describing data and can become a computer program with graphic charts.

Bibliography

Bergson, Henri. **Time and Free will: an essay on the immediate data of consciousness**. Kessinger Publishing, LLC: Kila, MT.

Clarke, Adele. (2005). **Situational Analysis: Grounded theory after the postmodern Turn**. Sage Publications.

Canguilhem, Georges. (1989). **The Normal and the Pathological**. Urzone, Zone Books: New York.

Deluze, Gilles. (1993). **The Fold: Leibniz and the Baroque**. University of Minnesota Press,

Descartes. (1985). **The philosophical writings of Descartes**. Translated by Cottingham, Stoothoff, Murdoch. Cambridge University Press.

Leibniz, G, W. (1998). **Philosophical texts.** Translated by Richard Franks and R. S. Woolhouse. Oxford University Press.

Rise, Guenter. (1999). **Mending Bodies, Saving Souls: A History of Hospitals.** Oxford University Press.

Theoharis, Sotiria. (2013). **Life with breast cancer: timing medical intervention.** Create-space.

-----. (2015). **Society from discrete numbers to infinity**. Create space.

Zizek, Slavoj. (1991). **For they know not what they do: Enjoyment as a Political Factor.** Verso: London New York.